PICTURE CROSSWORD PUZZLES

Deb T. Bunnell

DOVER PUBLICATIONS, INC.
Mineola, New York

Note

In these fun-to-do crossword puzzles, the clues are not *words,* but *pictures*! To do the puzzle, look at the crossword grid space marked 1; the picture marked 1 is your clue to the word that goes in that space. Go on then to the space marked 2 and to picture 2, continuing through all the numbered spaces until you've done them all. Look carefully at the picture clues. Sometimes the word is illustrated not by the whole picture, but a part of it (shown by an arrow). And when you've finished the puzzle, have fun coloring the pictures.

Solutions for all the puzzles are on pages 29–31.

Bibliographical Note

This Dover edition, first published in 1999, is a republication of the puzzles from *Picture Cross-Word Puzzles* by George Carlson, The Platt & Munk Co., New York, 1958. The illustrations have been newly prepared especially for this edition.

International Standard Book Number: 0-486-40798-5

Manufactured in the United States of America
Dover Publications, Inc., 31 East 2nd Street, Mineola, N.Y. 11501

3

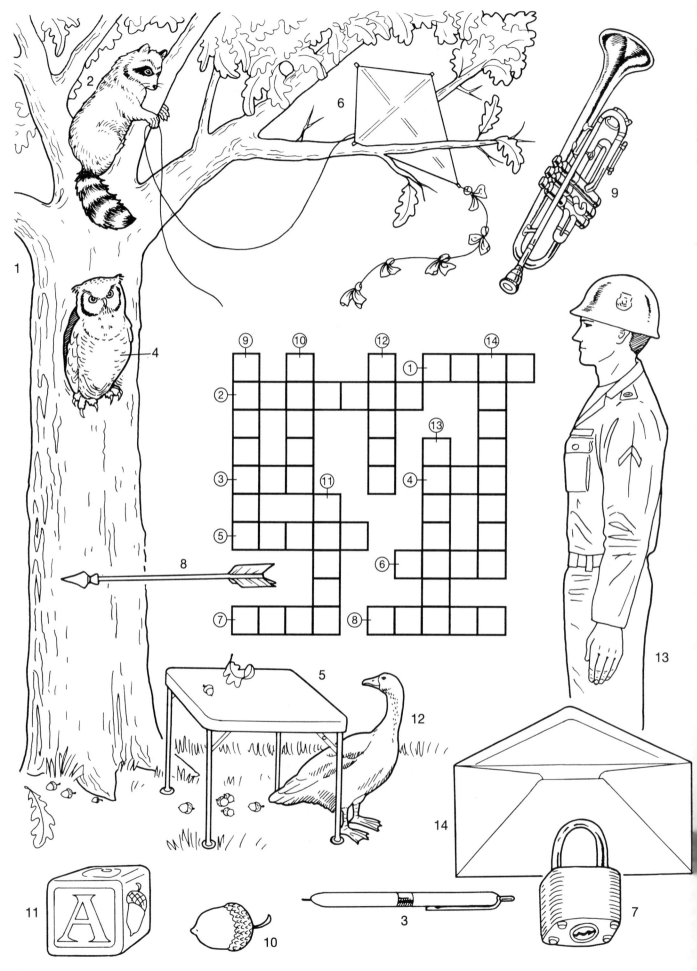

6

7

TOYS AND GAMES

15

16

18

25

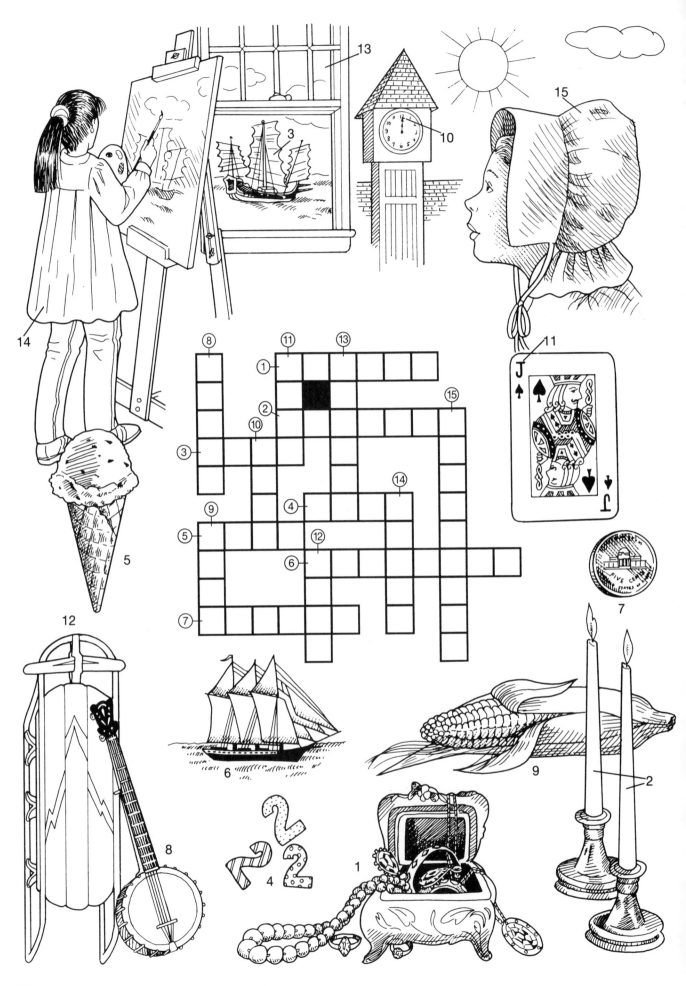

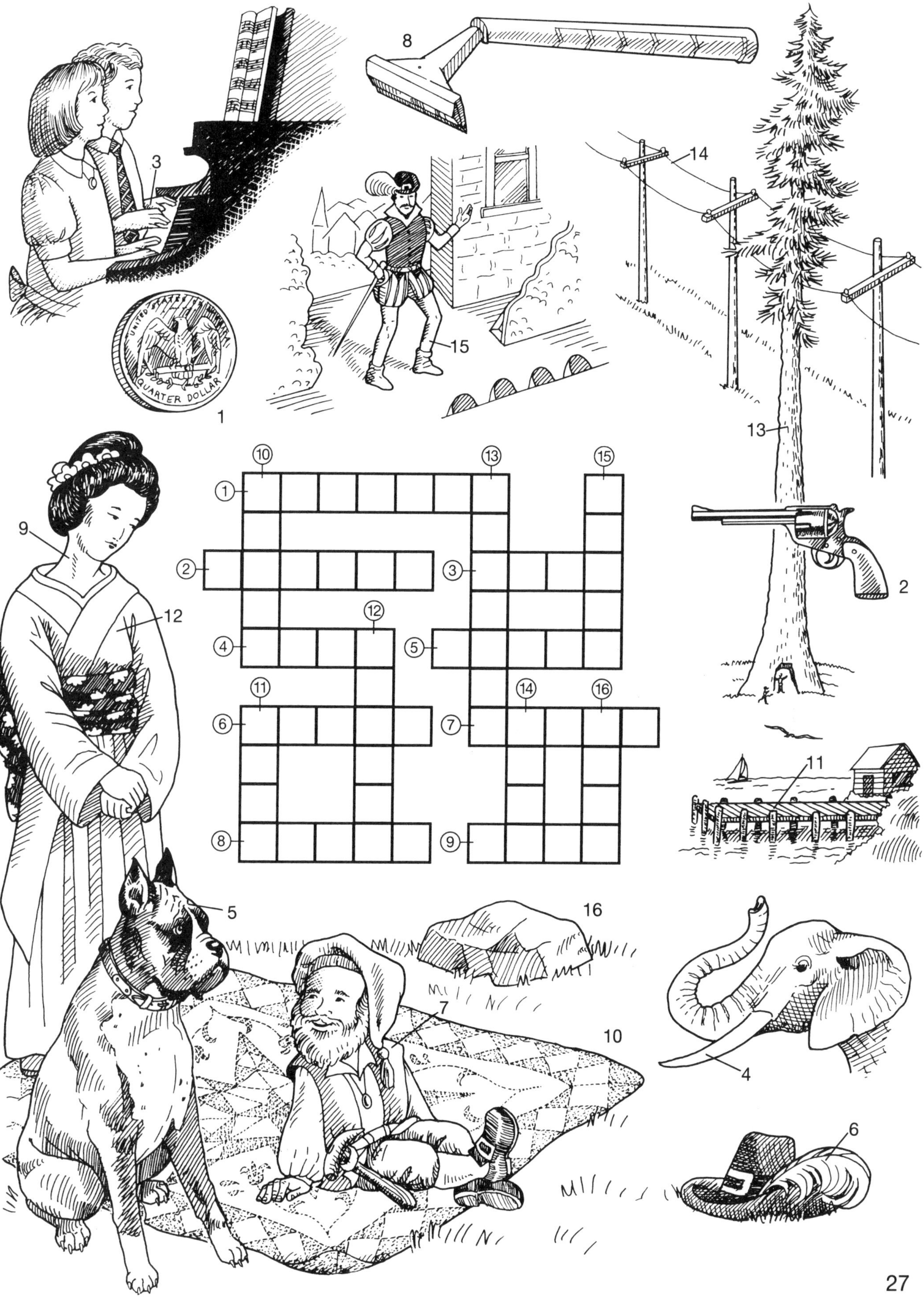
QUARTER DOLLAR

Solutions

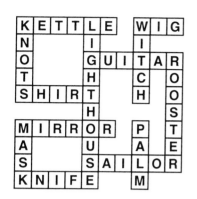

page 3

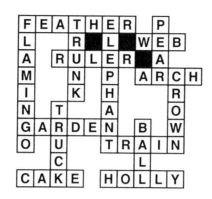

page 4

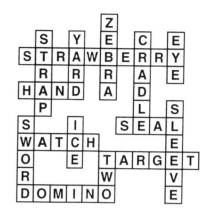

page 5

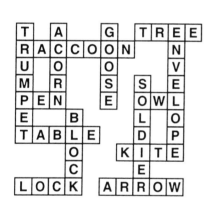

page 6

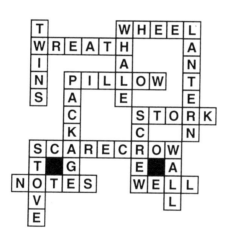

page 7

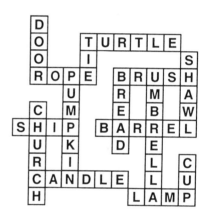

page 8

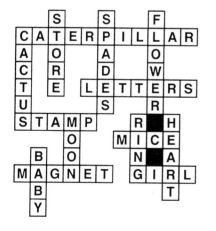

page 9

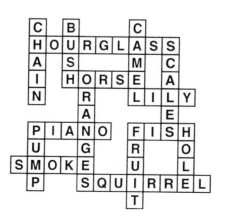

page 10

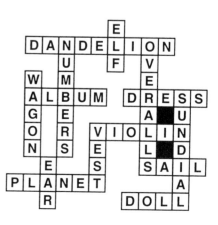

page 11

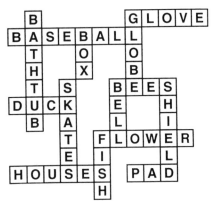

page 12

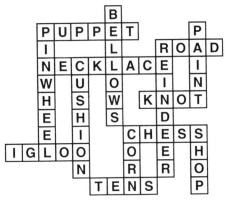

page 13

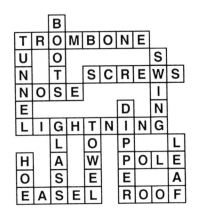

page 14

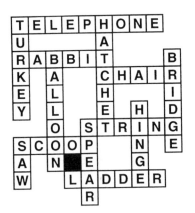

page 15

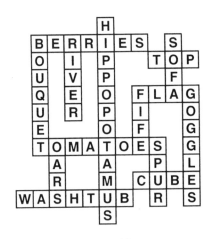

page 16

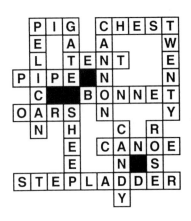

page 17

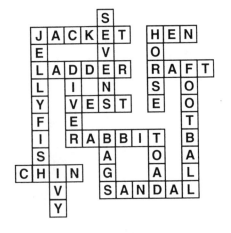

page 18

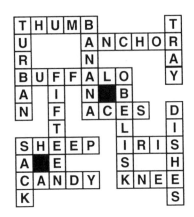

page 19

page 20

page 21

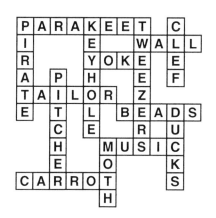

page 22

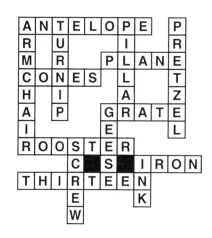

page 23

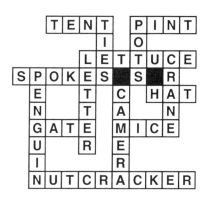

page 24

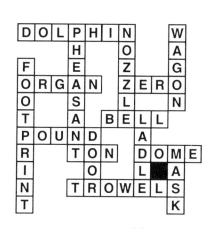

page 25

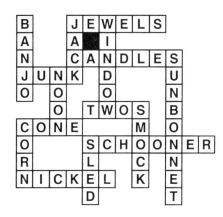

page 26

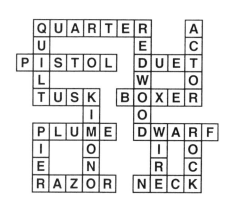

page 27

page 28